Hillary Wilson
2018

This Journal

BELONGS TO

_____

Life itself is a work of art

Feeling connected to the state of being alive is what fuels my desire to create. My passion for art and creativity comes from a deep, foundational love of new and familiar experiences, a reverence for the rich and boundless wonder of nature, and the joy of exploring what it means to be human. It can be easy to take these things for granted.

I often find myself thinking that there must be more to life than living it. Some may find comfort in this idea, but for me, there is greater comfort in the baseline simplicity of life and beauty in the hidden complexity of nature and the human experience. So many different things had to occur for me to exist. There doesn't need to be more. I have one human body. I exist at this moment in time. The passage of time and changes within and around my body are the only guarantees.

In many ways, art is a bridge between what I see and what I feel, both physically and emotionally. I find it nearly impossible to separate the two in my interpretation of the world. It's one thing to know it's springtime and another thing entirely to see the sun filtering through fresh and delicate new leaves on a spring morning, to be aware of each tree's state of growth, or to notice how the air feels when there are rustling leaves.

I try to be present in the emotions life brings and express them in ways others can connect with. Connecting with my emotions and those of the people around me is a central part of what drives me to create. Art serves as a way to communicate without explicitly telling the viewer what they should think or how they should feel.

With Love and Warmth,

Hillary

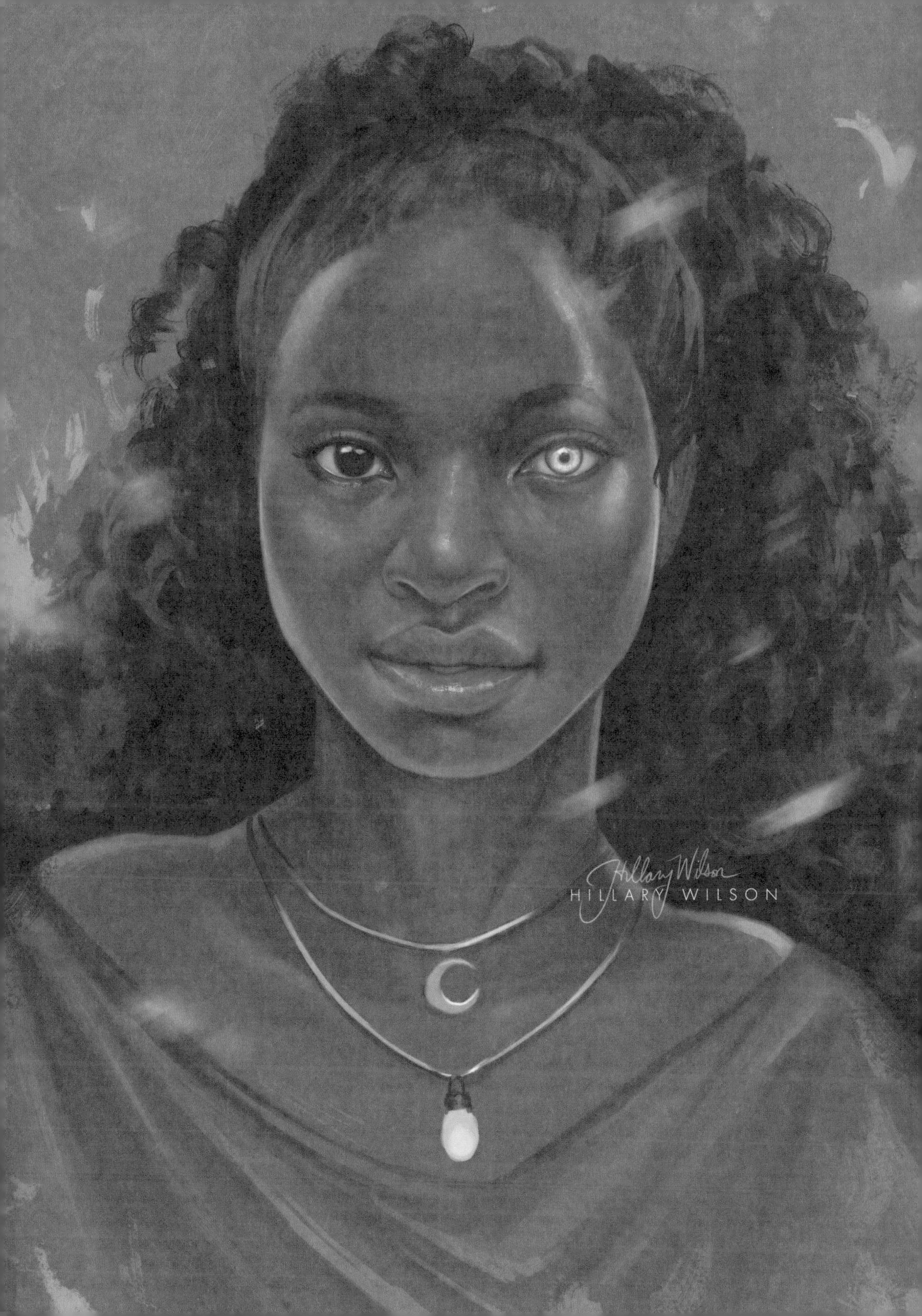
HILLARY WILSON

HILLARY WILSON

Science & Spirituality

Scientific learning and understanding help me feel connected to life and nature. For me, it's a deeply important spiritual tool. My sense of connectedness to all things has become more poignant and nuanced the more I've learned, understood, and engaged with life as a student of science. This might sound contradictory to some. How can one maintain feelings of awe and reverence for life when science strips away the mystery and magic?

That science and magic are entirely separate is a common misconception. Science has deepened my sense of connectedness and enriched my life. Questioning everything, asking how and why, has grounded me spiritually and intrigued me intellectually.

I often find science, the act of questioning, imagining, and incrementally testing, more exciting, complex, and mysterious than anything else I can imagine. When I know more about a topic, I'm better able to understand how it connects to other things. I ask questions that ever deepen my understanding. Take plants and herbs, for example. Most of us know they have different uses depending on the application. However, understanding why plants and herbs have those unique properties ushers in a new world of appreciation for them. Many serve functions, such as helping the plant grow, attracting pollinators, repelling or killing pests, or helping to maintain their environment. Understanding these properties and isolating and replicating their chemical compounds has led to the development of many medicines and treatments. That's pretty magical to me.

What is cough syrup, if not a potion? What is a tablet of medicine, if not a magical powder that has been compressed into a more usable form? What is a caffeinated beverage if not a draught of energy and wakefulness? Chemistry is essentially a potions class. Science, in many ways, is magic. It opens the door of wonders to the mystery and strangeness of life.

————————————————————

HILLARY WILSON

Fantasy

I've loved fantasy themes since I was a child. The bending of reality is a great way of expressing imagination and creativity. It encourages questions like, what if? and why? It invites you to view the mundane through the lens of magic and transform the ordinary in fresh, exciting ways, with only as many constraints as you choose.

Fantasy is potential. It's the potential to take the constraints and challenges life throws at us and find new ways to process, disregard or overcome them.

WHAT WOULD YOU LIKE TO LOOK AT THROUGH A MAGICAL LENS?

My love for science is deeply entwined with my love of fantasy. Ideas for possible worlds, magical systems, and stories come to me when I am inspired by something scientific, whether in a book, journal article, or documentary.

Inspiration comes in many forms, from the magical to the mundane. Embracing the fantastical brings magic to the everyday.

The Line Between Science & Magic

Many marvels that were once considered acts of magic are now supported with scientific evidence. We can break them down into their smallest, most fundamental parts. We understand their composition, their origin, their reasons for existing. That doesn't mean there isn't magic in their makeup.

Taking a pill and having pain vanish, predicting the weather, witnessing the majesty of an aurora borealis or a solar eclipse: Are these signs of magic, or are they science? What makes something science and not magic?

Does magic become science when we understand its components and how they fit together to make a whole? In that case, could an untested scientific hypothesis be considered magic? If you know the ingredients for a magical remedy and the healing properties of each component, is that different from knowing the active ingredients in a medication? Why does something do anything anyway?

Is something magic when it inspires awe, wonder, and excitement for the unknown? What if science also does that? Maybe a doctor becomes a mage when you substitute a white coat for a white cloak. Perhaps a compound becomes a potion when you take it from an Erlenmeyer flask and put it in a decorative bottle.

Perhaps science is magic with more steps. Maybe science is magic stripped to the bones.

To me, science and magic are two sides of the same coin. Seeking evidence for how something works isn't the antithesis of magic, just like awe and imagination aren't the antitheses of science. Magic is science seen through a lens of wonder.

———————————————

It's Just Skin

Life is simple, yet so complex. Everything around us—from weather cycles that span continents to the microscopic bacteria that thrive in our bodies—exists as its own infinitely complex system.

Feeling connected to the simplicity of life, while appreciating how deeply complex life can be in serving its biological purpose to survive and thrive, encourages balance in creative pursuits. Understanding the workings of something helps me connect to its nature, which motivates me to create.

SKIN DEEPLY INSPIRES ME.

Skin is the largest organ of the body. It comes in many different shades and textures. My skin isn't just a simple, brown dressing for muscle and bone. It's so much more than that. Its multiple layers of specialized cells are interspersed with nerves and vessels to form an effective barrier between vulnerable tissue and the external world. My skin is brown because cells called melanocytes produce organelles called melanosomes, which hold tiny pigment particles called melanin. These particles are more plentiful and hang around for longer than they would if my skin wasn't brown. These melanin particles form a haze over the nuclei of my skin cells, shielding them and the DNA inside them from the sun's radiation. So much is happening just below the surface of my body. But also, it's just skin.

That my skin is brown is a fundamentally neutral fact, but this neutrality is beautiful. My skin is what it is. It has specific functions and adaptations. Some skin offers greater protection from the sun. Other paler shades lack sun protection but are great at using the sun's rays to make vitamin D. Some skin has freckles. Some skin gets dry easily. Some skin is smooth. Some is rough. Some is aged. Some has been damaged, healed, and formed scar tissue. All skin types and shades are beautiful despite their differences. No matter what type of skin a person has, it serves a purpose and tells a story.

The Inherent Neutrality of the Body

I take comfort in the idea that most things in life are fundamentally neutral: neither good nor bad, positive nor negative. This includes the body.

The body connects us to the physical world and allows us to experience a plethora of emotions that enrich our lives and keep us healthy.

I don't see any human as inherently better or worse because of their unique characteristics. If someone is blind, they simply don't have vision. They are a human with a body that can do certain things, but not others. No individual human body can do everything, and that's okay. As humans, as creatures that do better as a group, our strength comes from sharing our skills and benefiting from the different things that others can do.

The ebb and flow of my emotions give me important information about my inner equilibrium. Over the years, I've had several struggles with my health that took a toll on me, physically, mentally, and emotionally. It is tempting to blame yourself or view your struggles as a failure when you are struck by sudden hardship or sickness. Experience has taught me to avoid attaching morality to my health, my body's state, or its current capabilities. If I am injured or sick, it may be tragic, it may be something for me to adapt to or overcome, it may cause sadness, confusion, or anger, but my body is still my own. It isn't worth less because of its sickened or weakened state.

Sometimes the state my body is in requires me to get help from those around me, and that's okay. Though it can be difficult, I do my best to appreciate every moment, even if I don't enjoy each one. I'm grateful for every day I can walk, run, stand, and balance on one foot. If I live to old age, many of these abilities will fade. I could lose them even sooner. Needing help, assistance, or accommodation doesn't make someone less dignified, less worthy, or less human. Needing help is just a part of being human in a changing body, in a changing world.

To be human is to live to the fullest extent possible, to use my body for what it's designed to do, to the best of its ability. I'm grateful for the attributes that not only help me survive and navigate the world but add to the richness of my life:

- My muscles, which help me move, play sports, lounge comfortably around the house, and pet cute dogs.

- My hearing, which allows me to listen to music, appreciate birdsong, and enjoy the rustle of wind through the trees.

- My vision, which helps me create art, read books, and wonder at the beauty of a flower in bloom.

- My sense of smell, which lets me appreciate the aromatic experience of teas and herbs, the complexity of perfumes and spices.

- My nerves, which keep me safe from harm by alerting me to pain and temperature extremes, and let me enjoy a hug.

Living means using my body's senses to keep myself alive. It also means enjoying life while I'm living it, using my senses for play, for creative inspiration. The body is an inherently neutral vessel, shaped by circumstances outside our control and the choices we have made. It is neither good nor bad — it simply is.

————————————————

Projection

I work hard to authentically and respectfully engage with other people and cultures, but it can be tricky to avoid projecting my preconceived ideas onto them. If I don't fully understand something, my feelings about it are generally based on guesses and assumptions specific to my culture. Though projection is a necessary part of empathy, if I do it too much, I run the risk of only engaging with ideas familiar to myself rather than the true nature and story of another. My story is my story. My experiences are my experiences. No one else has had the same ones. It can be difficult to communicate effectively with people when I lose sight of that.

It's impossible for me to separate a creation from those who brought it into being because it wouldn't exist without them. Engaging with other people and their stories is a privilege. A singular object or tradition is the culmination of many people's efforts, the ancestors who paved their path, and the stories that shaped them. I am always grateful for the opportunity to engage with something or someone new.

_____

Hillary Wilson
HILLARY WILSON

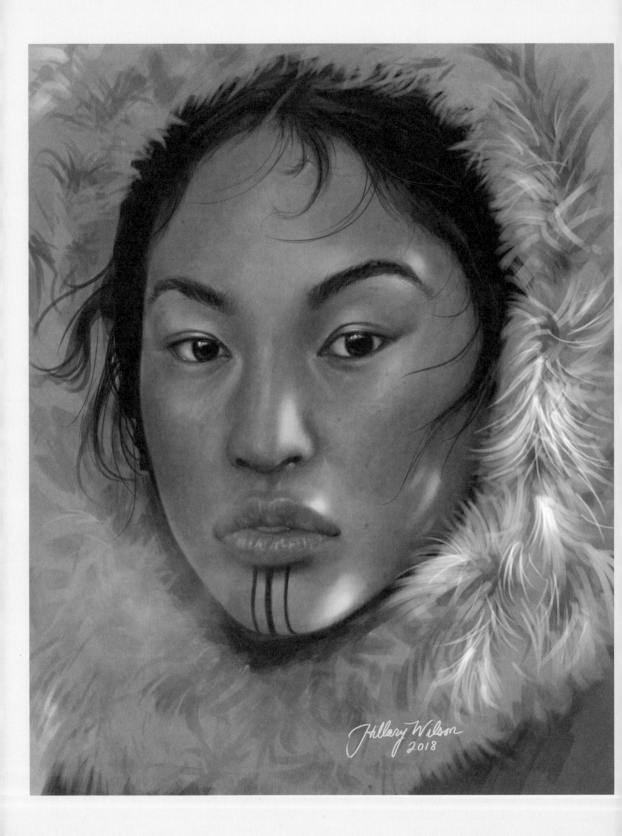

Hillary Wilson
2018

Masculinity & Femininity

Much of my artistic expression is shaped by my interpretation of my femininity. I'm fascinated by the social concept of masculinity and femininity. Part of that probably comes from how deeply complex our connections to those things are and how difficult it can be to define them in ways that feel real or hold any sort of truth.

I don't really see masculinity and femininity as something confined by or defined by gender or sexuality. I see it more as a spectrum, juxtaposing elements in ways that are complementary. Ideals of femininity and masculinity are deeply intertwined with culture, upbringing, and a host of intangible factors. I think everyone can display

shifting degrees of either or both. Neither is better or worse than the other.

Cultural norms are always changing, so it's hard to put a finger on what is strictly masculine or feminine. My preferred gender expression is more on the feminine side, but I also think many of my associations with femininity stem from the culture I've been steeped in. My actions trend more traditionally feminine if my clothing is feminine, but I don't feel it detracts from my femininity if I'm wearing more masculine clothing. I enjoy flowy dresses, jewelry, flowers, and pastel colors because I like them, not necessarily because I think they make me more feminine. At the end of the day, is there any reason why those things are considered feminine? I don't think so. Fabric is fabric. Jewelry has been a symbol of self-expression and status for all genders in many cultures throughout history. Flowers can have male parts, female parts, or both. I'm sure that someone from a different culture or upbringing would perceive my femininity differently, but I don't mind. No matter what, there will always be someone who perceives things differently from me. There will always be someone who perceives me differently.

For every rule about masculinity or femininity, there will always be exceptions. Humans can be difficult to define neatly. We are all such interesting and unique canvases for our cultures and experiences.

Do I even need to define what makes someone masculine or feminine? Probably not. I don't think it matters either way, and that's okay. As an artist, I can enjoy the different ways humans express themselves through masculinity, femininity, and every other interpretation of themselves. The more I leave my mind open to possibilities, the more inspired and creative I feel.

———————————————

HILLARY WILSON

Finding Balance in the Positive & Negative

I tend to feel alienated in spaces that project too much positivity or negativity.

To be positive when a situation doesn't call for it feels forced, inauthentic, and unsafe to me. I liken it to a door being slammed and hearing the lock click on the other side. It can hinder introspection and prevent the clear communication of one's boundaries and needs. It can make it challenging to process negative situations and act in ways that prioritize health and safety.

On the flip side, to be overly negative feels depressing, hostile, and similarly unsafe. It can make it difficult to be present and engaged in the moment. It can also make it hard for those who struggle with insecurity or doubt to take action, advocate for themselves, and summon the courage to remove themselves from a situation. Taking risks or speaking up is a challenge when undue negativity makes everything feel insurmountable.

Many hold high regard for positivity, but I sometimes struggle with the pressure to be positive. I don't think of myself as a purely positive or negative person. I strive to be peacefully neutral and perhaps gently hopeful. My goal is to strike a balance between positivity and negativity.

The negative parts of my story have driven many of my works that have truly spoken to people. Positivity is easier for me to sustain when I have adequately processed the negative. Sometimes the negative is still negative after I have confronted it, and that's okay. I can understand my worth, maintain my boundaries, and be better prepared to communicate those things in the future. In some cases, I feel empowered in the understanding that I am allowed to feel anger or sadness.

Art as an Activity versus a Skill

When it comes to art, the lines between activity, expression, and skill can get blurred.

Art is an activity, and as with all activities, repetition allows you to learn new skills and raise your standard. That doesn't mean there's no value or joy in doing it in an "unskilled" way.

As a child, I spent hours drawing with my sister. We would create stories and silly scenarios together. We had no concept of beauty or skill. We just had fun expressing our interpretations of the world.

I often mourn the ability to create art with others in a carefree, childlike way.

There's joy and exploration in being an amateur, a hobbyist, someone who does art for the sheer fun of it, regardless of skill. In many ways, now that I have so many expectations attached to my art, it's difficult for me to fully and freely express myself through it, even though learning and honing new skills has supposedly made creating art 'easier' for me. My eye for mistakes developed as my skill improved, so it's difficult to detach myself from expectations, even when they interfere with my creativity. I often get wrapped up in thinking, *I need to be better at a particular thing, or I need to practice this or that more.* I can't paint something ugly or bad.

I think many people feel as though art would be more fun if they were better at it. If they could just paint or draw this one thing perfectly, they'd be a 'proper' artist who creates in a state of ecstatic joy. In some ways, this is true. However, thinking about art that way can become a slippery slope that robs one of the joys of creating. Artistic improvement can be subtle and difficult to track. No matter one's skill or mastery, they will always think more can be improved.

My artistic skills have improved drastically from when I was a child, but I can't say that has shielded me from doubt or frustration. I've enjoyed art at every skill level, from when I struggled to draw people with correct proportions to being able to paint a realistic portrait from imagination. The subject matter I can easily paint has broadened, the positive feedback I receive for my artwork has increased, but I still feel frustrated sometimes. I still see so many areas I could improve. I still have to remind myself that I can have fun right now, even if my work isn't perfect.

Hillary Wilson

An Art Piece is a Journey

I often feel as though art isn't an intentional process. There's an element of discovery and a lack of complete control of the process that's interesting to consider. When an idea or thought is expressed through art, there's a point when the intangible must become tangible, and a person's inner world gets constrained by the medium they are using and their ability to manipulate it. I might have an idea in my head of what I want to paint, but the act of painting it, of holding a pencil, brush, or stylus, moving my hands, and making decisions about the colors and lighting, tends to lead the painting down paths that I didn't plan. Even when I spend a lot of time planning an illustration and making conscious decisions the entire time I create it, I still end up having a moment where I realize that the work is coming together beyond my control. The artistic process can sometimes feel like trying to redirect a rushing river. I do my best to direct the flow, but it will never be wholly within my control.

_____

Hillary Wilson
HILLARY WILSON

Gratitude & Mindfulness

For much of my life, I've heard people talk about the importance of gratitude as a tool for being more content in life and the present moment. I've often found it challenging to pin down exactly what that means for me. It was tough to put this concept into practice in a meaningful way for a long time. Though I recognized the positive things in my life, I had trouble feeling wholeheartedly connected to those things in the moment.

Diving deeply into what the positives in my life mean to me—focusing on how they influence me as the particular human I am, with the particular body I have, with the particular perspective I hold—finally allowed me to feel more gratitude and appreciate being in the moment.

One of the things I am grateful for is the ability to move my body. Exercise is essential to my physical and mental health. I find that exercising grounds me, helps regulate my emotional responses, and forces me to feel connected to my body. If I go for a run, I try to feel joy and gratitude in the fullness of that experience. I dwell on the sensations of my body as it changes to accommodate the action of running in the present moment and over time. How my body reacts varies with the seasons, whether it's hot, cold, dry, or humid. When I run consistently, my body grows certain muscles, changes the way my heart responds to the work, and forms calluses on the balls of my feet and the pads of my toes. If I lift weights consistently, my body sends resources to different muscles and I get calluses on my palms from gripping the weights.

My body is a complex collection of different systems that regulate themselves and each other and respond to the environment and the demands being placed on them. When I break down my actions or state of being and truly sit with what I am experiencing in the moment, I often feel less anxious or worried. I've had my fair share of health issues throughout my life, some of which I'm still managing. It can be hard to avoid placing pressure on myself and my body, but when I redirect my focus from what should or could have been and focus on responding to my environment and what is, I become capable of gratitude.

———————————————————————

The Beautiful Practicality of Emotions

It can be easy to fall into the habit of viewing emotions as inherently indulgent, irrational, or impractical, as things to be ignored in favor of an unattainable emotionless state. For me, emotions are important mechanisms and complex signals that alert me to things that need more attention.

Emotions can give us a wealth of information about how our life choices and past and current experiences affect us overall. They can be a catalyst for more profound thought and exploration, like how physical pain can alert someone to danger, injury, or illness. If I touch something hot and it hurts me, I know to exercise caution with similar things or to rearrange my surroundings, so I'm less likely to hurt myself. If I feel pain somewhere in my body, it's usually a sign that I should pay attention and figure out what's causing it. Even if it's just telling me that I should rest for a day, that signal is grounded in a useful mechanism for my survival.

When something feels wrong or upsets me, it prompts me to question myself: *Why am I feeling this way? Should I advocate for myself and my needs? Should I adjust my expectations or remove myself from this situation?* When I see my emotions as signals, I take a moment to stop, think, journal, and figure out where they are coming from.

ONCE I'VE UNDERSTOOD MYSELF, I CAN ACT AS NEEDED.

This isn't to say that any time I feel a strong emotion, I assume it is justified. For example, I may feel distraught about a perceived slight from my partner, but after paying attention to that signal and journaling about it, I understand why I felt that way. I may realize that I was associating the signal with a previous experience that caused me to perceive my partner more negatively and misread his intent. In a case like that, understanding why I have that response and effectively communicating with my partner about my feelings and my needs, rather than blaming him for my response, can help resolve the issue and ensure we are both understood. My emotional response was valid, even if it wasn't entirely justified, and listening to it alerted me to a need to communicate.

Depression, which I have struggled with for much of my life, is another example. I've grown to realize that when I am in a depressed state, my emotions are still valid even when they do not accurately reflect my life, relationships, and surroundings.

You are at your most vulnerable in a depressive state. Emotions and stresses that feel manageable when mentally healthy feel cataclysmic when depressed. I can recognize my negative emotions as symptoms, as a sign that something needs attention, the same way I would if I was in physical pain or discomfort. If I can recognize my triggers for depression, I can take action and better manage it. Maybe I need to ask for more support from the people who love me. Perhaps I need to be gentler with myself during my workday. Sometimes, being mindful of what is happening and adjusting what I do can help get me through it. At other times, I may need to seek professional support.

———————————————————————

The Human Paint Smear

I like to look at humanity as a big paint smear. The colors blend and merge to form new colors and shades, but you can still see the individual colors in many places. Someone can look like they fit a particular color family, but there are many shades, tints, and temperatures within that family, and the different colors can blend.

To take the paint analogy further, though someone may have specific associations with a color, one cannot objectively say that one color is better or worse than another. Each color has its place, purpose, and beauty. If you were to cut one color from your palette completely, call it ugly or act like it doesn't exist, you would miss out on a range of beautiful and unique blends.

_____

Jillary Wilson
2019

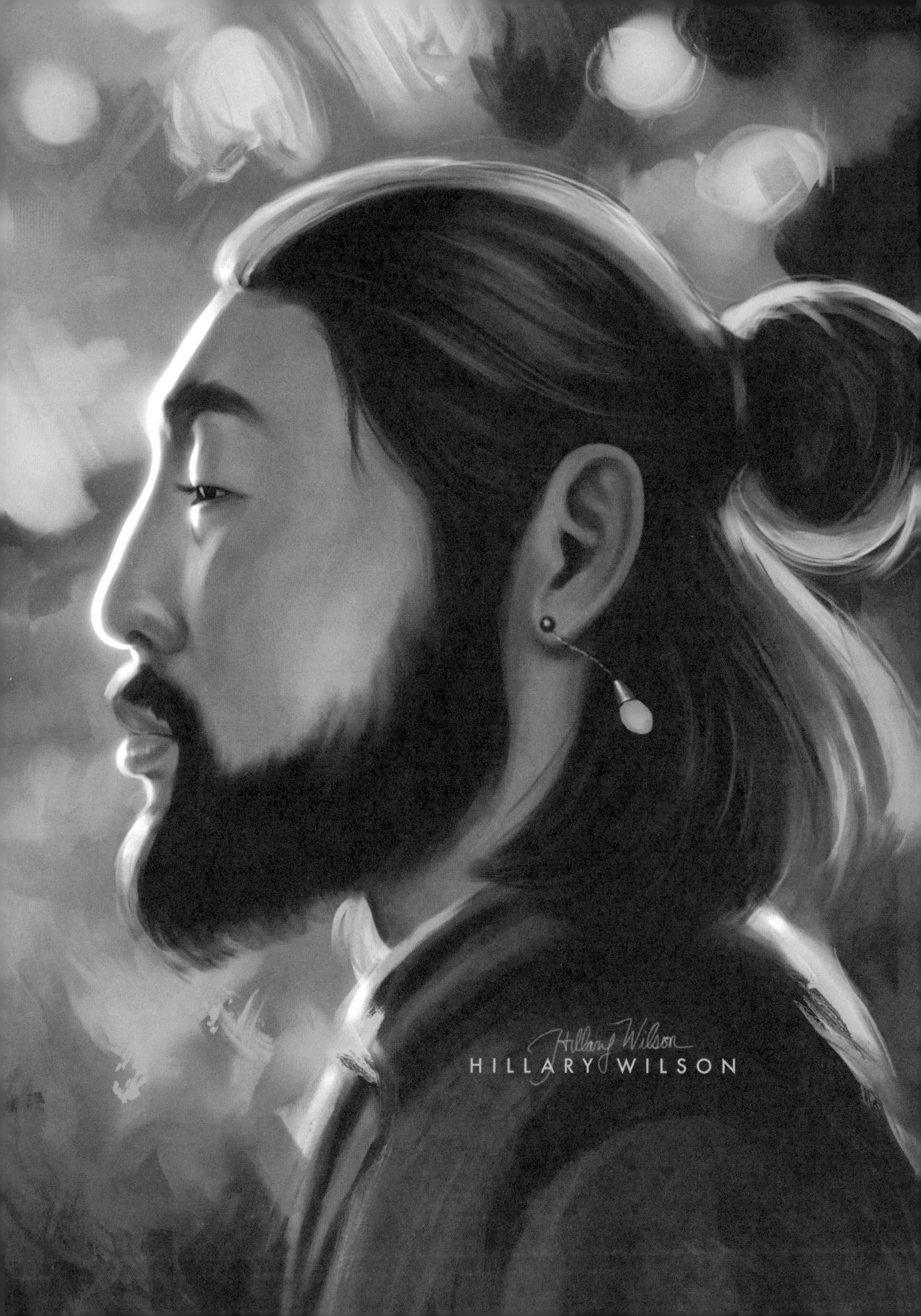
Hillary Wilson
HILLARY WILSON

Appreciate Your Features

People's features are a constant source of artistic inspiration for me. There are endless variations in human faces and bodies. A person's features hint at their story and their ancestry. I love distinct features. I love that there are large noses, small noses, hooked noses, wide noses, noses with high bridges, noses that tilt upwards, and noses with wide nostrils. I love that there are people with skin the color of volcanic glass and others with hair the color of sunflowers. There are people with long, willowy limbs and people with broad barrel chests.

Humanity's capacity for variation is a gift. I would have much less to explore and be delighted by as an artist if we weren't so varied.

May relatives on my mother's side have a particularly strong and full hairline. We also share a distinct mouth shape, and many of us have a unique tone to our voices. My mother's parents were Jamaican immigrants, and several times in my life, when I have seen someone who has a similar hairline, mouth, or voice, I also discovered that they or part of their family has come from Jamaica.

I grew up knowing very little about my heritage and ancestors. My immediate family was close and loving, but a connection to my ancestry wasn't a heavy factor in my upbringing. Despite this, the reality of who I am is a direct continuation of those who came before me. My nose was given to me by my father. My skin tone, eye color, and hair color and texture are gifts my parents and ancestors gave me when they gave me life.

Many people have complicated and tumultuous relationships with their features and traits, especially those belonging to marginalized racial groups and ethnicities. Throughout my childhood, outside my home and family, I fought the unfortunate external feedback that subtly and explicitly suggested my features were somehow lesser. However, if my skin was not brown and my nose was not wide, I would have different parents and a different history. I would no longer be myself.

Each person's features tell a distinct story. Their features are a reflection of what came before. The story would be different if they had other ancestors. I can't change who I am, but that is not something I wish for. I want to accept and acknowledge all parts of myself and my story: the good and triumphant, the difficult and tragic. I want to accept all those who came before me as they were and all those who walk beside me as they are.

_____

Author Bio

Hillary was raised in North Carolina by an endlessly supportive, adventure-loving family who encouraged every creative and educational pursuit she put her mind to. She received a master's degree in medical illustration from the Johns Hopkins School of Medicine in 2018. Combining her medical illustration background with her love for fantasy, wonder, and emotional connection, Hillary strives to celebrate the wonder of life, nature, and being human. She is particularly invested in exploring the rich variation in humanity and its implications on how we view ourselves and others. Hillary values storytelling and strives to balance the scientific and spiritual. In her day-to-day life, she freelances full-time.

www.hdwilsonart.com